What a delight 'Miss Sweetie Finds A Home' *is for cat lovers ... and those who wish they were! The natural, loving style of Rita-Marie's writing flows through the story, keeping the reader engaged and wanting to read more.*

It is the perfect accompaniment to a cuppa and time to relax. A story to appeal to all ages, it is light-hearted—yet it has a beautiful message about the connection between an animal and her humans.

Di Riddell
Author, Speaker, and Confidence Coach

I have been privileged to read 'Miss Sweetie Finds A Home' *about Rita-Marie's beautiful cat, Miss Sweetie, and the characters she comes into contact with.*

It is also a delightful story about the relationship between animals and humans, and the respect and love they have for each other.

I would recommend this book for anyone who loves their cat, to read about the ups and downs their families have around them.

Albina Porracin
Author, *Help Me! My finances are a mess*
Financial Counsellor and Coach

'Miss Sweetie Finds A Home' *is a lovely read. It provides an insight into the behavioural patterns of our fur-babies, and how privileged we are when they choose us to share their lives with us. This comes across really clearly through the antics of Miss Sweetie. I love that she is referred to as a nurse, because cats are also amazing 'service' pets, and are really in tune with our emotional needs, even if we are not. A great read for anyone wishing to learn more about feline fur-babies before adopting them and returning to their new 'forever' homes.*

Peta-Ann Wood
Holistic Coach,
Author, *What happens when they don't grow back: The upside-down view of life after a bilateral mastectomy*

MISS SWEETIE

FINDS A HOME

Rita-Marie Lenton

Miss Sweetie Finds A Home

Copyright © 2024 Rita-Marie Lenton

First published 2024

Rita-Marie Lenton
SoulCrystalEarth
32 Trafalgar Drive
Kippa-Ring QLD 4021 Australia
www.rita-marielenton.com.au

Self-published with technical guidance and support from Deborah Fay and the Authorpreneurs Bootcamp at Disruptive Publishing

Cover creation by Rita-Marie Lenton in Canva
Photographs supplied by Rita-Marie Lenton
Additional images sourced from Canva
Editing and layout by Jo Scott

All rights reserved. Without limiting the rights under Copyright reserved above, no part of this publication may be reproduced, stored in, or introduced into a database and retrieval system, or transmitted in any form or by any means (electronic, mechanical, photocopying, recording or otherwise) without the prior written permission of both the owner of the Copyright and the above publishers.

ISBN# 978-0-6456110-3-8 Print

ISBN# 978-0-6456110-4-5 Kindle

MISS SWEETIE FINDS A HOME

... and becomes the heart of a family

Rita-Marie Lenton

I dedicate this book to my husband David, my children Michael and Nerissa, my daughter-in-law Vali, and my beautiful grandchildren, Hannah, Ruby, and Hunter, who all challenged me to write something a bit more light-hearted, fluffy, and funny.

To the caring workers and volunteers at *Peninsula Animal Aid* for all their dedicated work looking after animals and finding new homes for them.

Last, but not least, to our 'Miss Sweetie' who everyday gives us a great sense of joy, amusement, and topics for my books.

CONTENTS

FOREWORD 1

PART ONE 3

PROLOGUE 5

MISS SWEETIE'S BEGINNINGS 9

GETTING TO KNOW HER NEW HOME 17

MEETING THE REST OF THE FAMILY 21

MISS SWEETIE, THE NURSE 27

FIRST SUMMER IN HER NEW HOME 33

MISS SWEETIE'S FIRST CHRISTMAS 37

MISS SWEETIE'S FIRST TIME ALONE 43

SETTLING INTO HER NEW HOME 47

MISS SWEETIE'S SECOND CHRISTMAS 51

MISS SWEETIE WELCOMING VISITORS 55

MISS SWEETIE'S THIRD CHRISTMAS 57

LIFE SETTLES INTO A ROUTINE 65

WHERE IS MY DAD? 71

PART TWO 81

THE CAT AND THE HOUSEKEEPER 83

MISS SWEETIE'S MANY QUALITIES 91

ABOUT THE AUTHOR..115

ACKNOWLEDGEMENTS...117

RESOURCES FOR ANIMAL RESCUE....................................119

MORE BY THE SAME AUTHOR..121

CONTACT RITA-MARIE LENTON...123

Foreword

Prepare to be charmed by the antics of the adorable Miss Sweetie, as you meet her in these pages.

She has had furry predecessors in Rita-Marie's house, but her place as the current reigning Queen is unchallenged.

Rita-Marie takes us on a gentle journey of the daily life of the beloved pet, Miss Sweetie. This dear little tabby cat and her busy life as a nurse, alarm clock, supervising foreman, and elf defensive line reflect the many ways our pets entwine themselves into our daily lives.

We love them being there, often underfoot or shamelessly demanding attention, and they love being in our midst—oblivious that they are often the glue that binds our pieces together.

Miss Sweetie claimed my heart from the first few pages, which only deepened as her story unfolded.

She will claim yours too.

Frances Cahill
Author
Your Kitchen Olympics and other remarkable athletic feats

PART ONE

The Pussycat

Prologue

Tabitha was just six weeks old when her human mum got her from the *Peninsula Animal Aid* rescue centre. On the day her mum found her she also adopted another kitten, Tigger; he was a few months older and ginger-coloured. How Tabitha loved her human family and her big brother Tigger! They had many good years living with each other.

Tigger was a big boy and Tabitha loved to torment him by running up the nearest palm tree, and because Tigger was so big, he could not run after her. Tabitha would make it to the top and stick her tiny head out through the fronds of the palm tree, and you could almost see her laughing as Tigger sat at the bottom of the tree wishing he could catch her.

Tigger   Tabitha

When Tigger became sick and crossed the 'Rainbow Bridge', Tabitha missed him terribly. She was lonely, but Tabitha still had her mum and dad, and they did their best to keep her company. As time passed, Tabitha grew older, but she still liked to run up and climb on the roof of the house and play chasey with the birds. She was safe, she had a good home, and she knew she was loved.

When COVID-19 struck in 2020 it was a trying time for everyone — including the animals. Tabitha knew she was not well, and she knew she would soon join her older brother, Tigger, across the 'Rainbow Bridge'.

As the time was drawing near, Tabitha sat with her dad in the front yard knowing they couldn't venture very far. She sat beside him and purred as she let him pat her. Tabitha was saying goodbye in her own way. She knew in her heart that her dad would not take her passing well.

Tabitha then came inside and went to bed. Her mum wished her good night and covered her with her favourite blanket. As the night became morning they found her at peace. She had gone to catch up with her brother, Tigger, once more so they could play chasey and frolic in the green meadows, just like they had so long ago.

Miss Sweetie's Beginnings

Miss Sweetie started her life as an orphan in the November of 2017.

She was a lucky kitten as she was sent to a nice place called *Peninsula Animal Aid,* a rescue centre where they had lots of luck at finding orphan pussycats a new home.

But as time went by, people came and went, and as Miss Sweetie grew, no one wanted to take her home.

Miss Sweetie did not mind so much; it was a comfortable place to stay, the carers took good care of her, and she was well fed.

Still, she dreamed of the day she would have a new home with a human family and a soft bed to lie on.

Then one night, when Miss Sweetie was sound asleep, she had a dream of another little tabby cat who came to her in spirit. The tabby cat shared with Miss Sweetie that she would no longer have to be in the refuge anymore, as a special family was finally going to choose *her!*

It was Easter Sunday morning when the human family found their little girl, Tabitha, had crossed the 'Rainbow Bridge'.

The human dad was so sad that he felt the need to look on the website of *Peninsula Animal Aid* at Redcliffe, because that was where they had found their little Tabitha, so long ago.

There was Miss Sweetie on the first page in all her glory: 'Sweetie by name and sweet by nature'. After much discussion with the human mum, a decision to contact the refuge was made.

It was during the COVID-19 pandemic, and the refuge had to be closed to the public. The new family stayed connected with the Redcliffe *Peninsula Animal Aid* every week to find out just when they would be allowed to pick Miss Sweetie up. Finally, the day arrived, and Miss Sweetie's new human family came to collect her.

That is, the dad came because the mum worked—so she was not at the house when Miss Sweetie was introduced to her new home.

Miss Sweetie's new human sister was there to greet her, and they got to know one another during that day.

Later that afternoon there was a noise outside. A car door slammed and a call came from outside the house. A voice could be heard asking, "Has the new pussycat arrived?" Miss Sweetie was startled, and she got scared and ran away, just sneaking a look from behind the couch.

There stood her new human mum, speaking to her softly, reaching out and trying to pat her. Miss Sweetie was very frightened of her human mum as she tried to pick her up. She was *so* scared she ran behind the couch again.

Miss Sweetie's new human mum tried to coax her out with food, but she wouldn't come out. Miss Sweetie was a real scaredy-cat!

Later that night when all was quiet, Miss Sweetie came out from her hiding place to find there was no one around, as they were all in bed. So, Miss Sweetie began to explore her new home.

She finally made her way into the human's bedroom, looked at the really big bed, and decided she would climb up and see her new human mum who was fast asleep.

When Miss Sweetie climbed onto her human mum's chest, she thought it made a good pillow so she sat down. Then her mum moved and woke up with a start. Poor Miss Sweetie got such a fright she ran away back into her hiding place!

Getting to know her new home

As the days went by, Miss Sweetie's human dad would spend lots of time with her. Miss Sweetie followed him everywhere.

Miss Sweetie still wasn't too sure about her human mum, though. Her mum wasn't mean, she was just not there all the time because she worked.

Miss Sweetie did learn that her mum would feed her when she got home from her work. But still Miss Sweetie didn't get close to her mum.

However, her mum didn't give up, she was very patient, and she kept trying to show Miss Sweetie affection.

Every now and then Miss Sweetie would notice that her new mum was a little bit sad, so she would jump onto her lap, and stay just for a few minutes ... but never with her face towards her mum!

Miss Sweetie's human mum would always bring her new toys to play with, and Miss Sweetie just loved the little plastic balls with the bells inside them. She would chase them around and play with them. This made her human family happy, and it always made them laugh.

Rita-Marie Lenton

Meeting the rest of the family

When Miss Sweetie first joined the family, she was aware of her human big sister, who did not live at the house all of the time. Then one day another set of humans arrived in a big car. The car door flung open and two little humans ran inside calling out, "Hello Granma!"

And to the shock and horror of Miss Sweetie, they had with them a furry dog named Diamond! Diamond was so excited to see Granma that she was jumping up all over Miss Sweetie's human mum. This was not something Miss Sweetie liked at all! No, sir— she was just not happy.

Miss Sweetie was to learn that the little humans, along with two big humans, were another part of her human family, and they had come to stay at the house. This time it was her human big brother, his wife, and their two children.

Once again, Miss Sweetie got very frightened and ran away and hid in her mum and dad's bedroom.

She stayed there all that day, and later that night when her mum called her for dinner the two little humans — known as the grandchildren — were sitting on the floor. They started to roll the balls towards Miss Sweetie; she liked that, and she started to play with them.

Over the next two days she got to know the grandchildren better.

However, Miss Sweetie did not like the furry dog called Diamond, and all Diamond wanted to do was play with her.

The next day Miss Sweetie's human sister came to visit. She liked her because she was someone she was familiar with and, along with the two little grandchildren, Miss Sweetie played with them all.

Then disaster struck! Another loud person arrived; this time it was another girl and she also bounced through the door saying, "Hello Granma", this startled Miss Sweetie, and once again she ran away. It was all too much, meeting all these humans who made up the bigger part of her human family.

When they all went home again Miss Sweetie settled back into her routine of exploring her new home with just her mum and dad.

Miss Sweetie liked it when her mum left for work, she would hop up on the couch with her dad and have a sleep with him.

When he got up and went outside to work, she would follow him out and she would sit with him. Miss Sweetie enjoyed watching him work, sometimes she even tried to help.

Miss Sweetie, the nurse

One day, Miss Sweetie woke to find her dad was getting ready with a little port to go to the hospital. Her mum went from the hospital onto work that day, and when she came home she made sure Miss Sweetie had her dinner. But Miss Sweetie was missing her dad, and she kept searching throughout the house looking for him.

After a while, Miss Sweetie's mum gently talked to her and explained her dad wasn't home, and that it was just the two of them.

Miss Sweetie looked at her mum and realised she was sad also, so she decided to sit on her chest, to give her mum some comfort—even though she still didn't understand why her dad wasn't home.

It was a few days later when her dad came home from the hospital with a very sore-looking knee. He could hardly walk. He had to use a walker to get around, and needed to practice walking every day. This was where

Miss Sweetie would hop on the walker to give her dad encouragement to walk around the house.

Miss Sweetie looked forward to the walks on the walker — it was like she was on a ride at the amusement park. Round and round the house they would go, with Miss Sweetie looking at her dad and encouraging him to keep going.

Then her dad had to use a skateboard while

sitting to help him practice moving his knee backwards and forwards. Miss Sweetie would sit and watch the process intently to make sure her dad was doing it right.

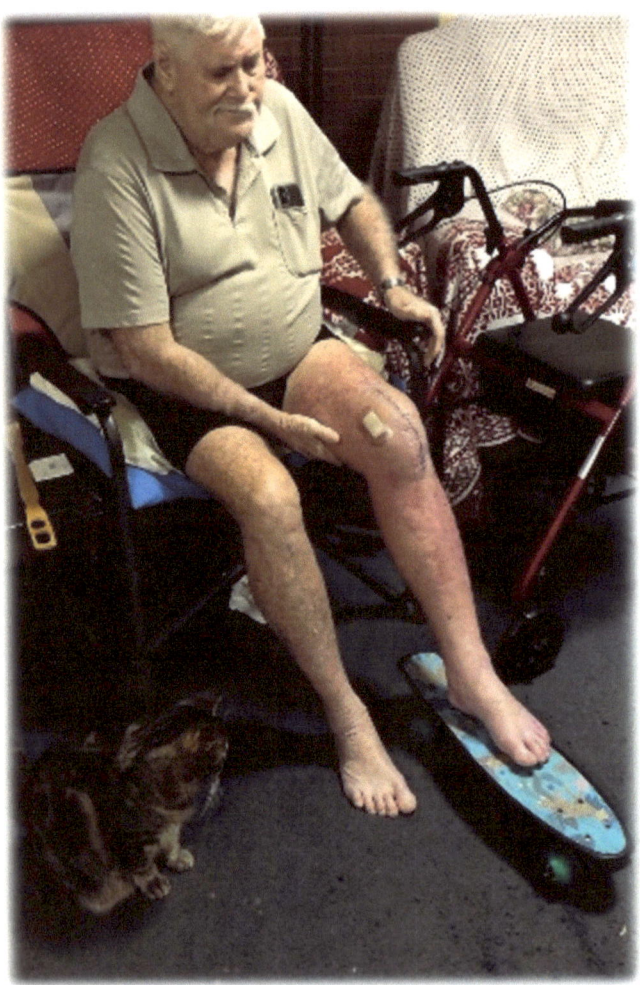

Miss Sweetie noticed her mum didn't go to work as much while her dad was sick. So, she started to watch what her mum was doing, and helped her by following her around the house as she did the housework and cooked the meals. It was fun sitting outside and getting to know her mum a lot more.

First summer in her new home

Spring was coming and Miss Sweetie's mum started working in her garden. Her mum had lots of lovely crystals, so Miss Sweetie loved to help put them in the garden for the full moon.

There were a whole lot of other areas to explore with her mum and dad. But Miss Sweetie never ventured too far from the house without them.

She soon learnt that they had a pool in the back yard, and as her mum and dad cleaned up the garden—getting it ready for the coming summer—Miss Sweetie loved to keep them company.

Miss Sweetie Finds A Home

Miss Sweetie's First Christmas

Strange things were happening around the house. Miss Sweetie's mum dragged out boxes from the cupboards and started to put pretty tinsel up everywhere.

And there was a tree with lots of pretty coloured baubles on it. Oh, my! Miss Sweetie had some fun trying to catch the tinsel before her mum got it on the tree. And didn't those baubles from the tree look tempting?

It was the night before Christmas, and all the presents were being put under the Christmas tree. Miss Sweetie wanted to get in and open them up. She sniffed them and patted them, and then Mum said, "NO!!"

Then the next week, once again there was all a commotion as the extra human family arrived—with that furry dog Diamond! Oh no, not again!

Miss Sweetie was back to hiding in the cupboard in her Mum and Dad's bedroom. The house was noisy as people came and went all day, and Miss Sweetie's mum couldn't convince her to leave the cupboard, so she put her litter tray in their bathroom and her food near the cupboard.

At night when the house was nice and quiet Miss Sweetie came out of the cupboard. She saw her mum and dad in bed and then she heard a noise. Oh no, that furry dog was in the house!

Diamond was sleeping in the back of the house, so once again Miss Sweetie decided that the cupboard was where she was going to stay. She was not coming out until they all went home again!

Miss Sweetie's First Time Alone

Miss Sweetie's humans were going away for the weekend, and they decided she would be safe enough to be left at home overnight on her own. Mum made sure she had cleaned up the litter tray, and she put out lots of fresh water and food so Miss Sweetie would not get thirsty or hungry.

Her mum and dad put the television on so Miss Sweetie would have company. And they put the air conditioner on so she wouldn't get too hot. They made sure all her favourite toys were around for her to play with, and then they were gone.

At first Miss Sweetie did not mind that she had her new home to herself, and she made sure she explored most of it without her mum and dad telling her she couldn't go into certain rooms.

When her mum and dad finally came home the next day, Miss Sweetie was very glad to see them again. She spent the rest of the day lying around on the lounge chairs with both her mum and dad, as they seemed to be exhausted from their weekend away with the rest of the human family.

Miss Sweetie Finds A Home

Settling Into Her New Home

Miss Sweetie had been with her new human family for almost a year now. She was getting more confident around her mum. Miss Sweetie would go outside for a little while on her own, but then ... something terrible happened!

Two birds decided they would let her know she wasn't welcome walking around outside, and they chased her! Miss Sweetie ran so fast she crashed through the open door, her hair standing on end, and she was trembling. Miss Sweetie was so frightened she did not go outside again for the rest of the week — even when her dad was with her.

One thing she *did* like about the outside was the pot of cat grass her mum bought for her, so she always enjoyed having a munch on the sweet grass shoots. Sweetie found it fun to chase the lizards, and her mum was always going mad at her for that.

Over the next twelve months, time went along pleasantly with Miss Sweetie getting more and more used to having the other humans come and go. She especially liked sitting outside with her dad every afternoon, waiting for her mum to come home.

Miss Sweetie knew that when her mum came home from work, it was dinner time. She liked dinner time, as this was her special time with her mum.

Then one day mum came home from work and said that she wasn't going back anymore, so she would have lots of time at home to play with Miss Sweetie now.

Oh no! That also meant her mum had time to take her to the vet!

Miss Sweetie's Second Christmas

Miss Sweetie's Mum had not been working full-time for a while now, so she would spend her days cleaning the house and sorting out the cupboards. Miss Sweetie loved to help by getting into those cupboards to see if everything was in order.

Miss Sweetie was also particular about making sure her mum vacuumed the floor correctly. She would watch her mum closely when it came time to clean out the litter tray. When her mum was finished, Miss Sweetie would get into the litter tray just to make sure it was properly cleaned out. Her mum referred to Miss Sweetie as *The Foreman*.

Then suddenly, a strange looking elf thing appeared — it seemed to pop up everywhere. Her mum sent photos to the grandchildren daily about this funny looking elf, and she mentioned the name 'Cinnamon Bread'. Miss Sweetie was not happy with this elf, as it seemed to be into all sorts of mischief. So, one day when her mum wasn't looking, Miss Sweetie caught the elf. "Oh, dear! You can't eat the elf!" said her mum, as she rescued it from Miss Sweetie's paws.

Then as fast as the elf seemed to appear, it disappeared on Christmas Eve. Miss Sweetie looked at her mum putting lots of presents under the tree again—they looked like so much fun. Miss Sweetie wanted to jump into the pile and play with them, but in her very stern voice, her mum once again said, "NO!"

Miss Sweetie Welcoming Visitors

Miss Sweetie learned that her mum and dad had visitors who liked to come and go. She was happy enough to hang around them, as long as there were no dogs!

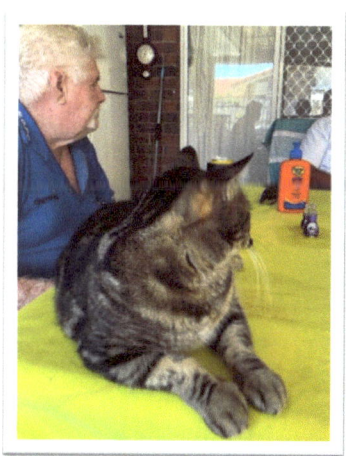

Miss Sweetie still loved to sit around with her dad and watch him work, sometimes she tried to help by biting the fishing line with which he was working to make a lure. She didn't understand why he never really wanted her to help.

Miss Sweetie's Third Christmas

Another year had passed, and suddenly things started to happen again. Miss Sweetie's mum was digging around in those boxes again, and out came the tinsel along with the Christmas tree. Miss Sweetie couldn't wait to get hold of all those Christmas baubles! Her mum was getting cranky at her dad as he kept getting the baubles and rolling them on the floor for Miss Sweetie to chase.

Then, lo and behold, in a flash we had a funny looking elf once again ! There was a note that read: *Cinnamon Bread* was staying with Santa as she was too scared of Miss Sweetie.

This time, in Cinnamon Bread's place, two elves arrived. One elf was dressed in black, and she was called 'Willow Woe'; and the other elf was dressed in red, and her name was 'Ruby Red Socks'.

Now Miss Sweetie was not sure if she liked them at all, as they kept taking over her bed. Every day Willow Woe seemed to be doing something bad to Ruby Red Socks, so Miss Sweetie pounced and got hold of Willow Woe, to give her a good shaking, especially because mum wasn't watching.

During the month of December, leading up to

Christmas Eve, Miss Sweetie couldn't help but notice all the mischief those elves got up to.

And every chance she got she would pounce on them when her mum wasn't watching.

Miss Sweetie didn't mind Ruby Red Socks. But Willow Woe made Miss Sweetie really mad when she tried to put Ruby Red socks into the oven, and then ... Willow Woe started to eat her cat biscuits!!

Christmas Day was much quieter that year, as the other family members didn't visit until after Christmas.

Then suddenly here they were again! The family arrived ... without Diamond this time. Miss Sweetie had a lot more fun with her family this time around. As they spent time together by the pool, she would watch the children playing in the swimming pool.

Miss Sweetie would follow the little ones around as they played with her. She was much happier getting to know this part of the family since they had left that furry dog at home!

* * *

Miss Sweetie often sits alone at the back door and looks out 'across the way'. And as the afternoon breeze gently comes from the east, she lifts her nose and smells the air. Her former home — the animal refuge — is 'across the way', and sometimes on that afternoon breeze she can smell her old, familiar home.

Miss Sweetie sniffs the air and takes a big breath, she pauses for just a moment, then turns around and comes back into the house, where she knows she is finally home.

Rita-Marie Lenton

Life Settles Into A Routine

Since the last Christmas, life had become more routine as Miss Sweetie followed her mum around the house, checking she had done the housework correctly. And making sure her dad was okay as he worked on the lures he was making.

But Miss Sweetie soon discovered there was another house guest, as the eldest granddaughter of the family came to stay.

Miss Sweetie didn't mind too much, because the eldest granddaughter 'came and went', and sometimes brought her friend to stay.

Miss Sweetie likes the friend because he plays with her. She really enjoys the company — especially when mum and dad go to visit their family who live down the coast.

The house just settled into a nice routine for a few months ... and then the eldest granddaughter moved out to a new home.

* * *

For the first half of the year in 2023 things were quiet and pleasant.

Then 'it' happened!

In July a big car with flashing lights came, and there were strange people in the house. Miss Sweetie's dad was lying on the big couch, her mum was scared and she was speaking with the extra people about what was happening to her dad.

Miss Sweetie was frightened and she ran behind the couch at first, then later she crept out to look at all the strange machines and bags on the floor. Then one of the people went outside and came back in with a strange looking bed to put her dad on.

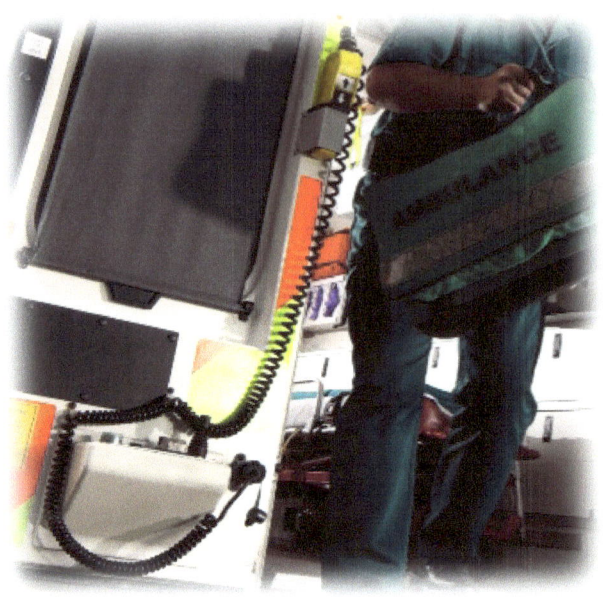

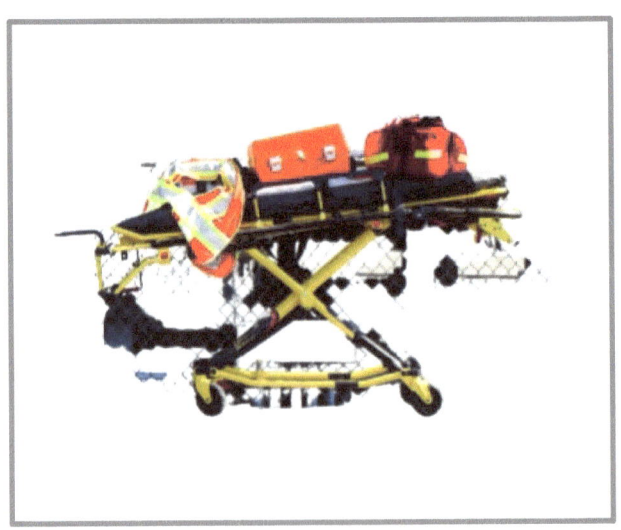

Miss Sweetie's mum looked really worried. She went outside to the big car with flashing lights, then when she came back inside she changed her clothes, put on her shoes, and grabbed her handbag. She patted Miss Sweetie on the head and then went out in the car.

Where Is My Dad?

When Miss Sweetie's mum returned in the early hours of the morning she was crying. Miss Sweetie hopped onto her lap to give her comfort, and as her mum patted her, she said "Miss Sweetie, we need to pray your dad is going to be okay."

The next morning Miss Sweetie's mum set about feeding her, then she got on the phone to the family to let them all know that dad had been taken to the hospital ... and it was serious.

Over the next two days Miss Sweetie's mum would come and go as she went to the hospital to sit with her dad. When her mum was home, Miss Sweetie would climb onto her lap and

Miss Sweetie Finds A Home

just look at her. Miss Sweetie just knew there was something wrong: Dad wasn't home, and Mum kept explaining he was in the hospital.

Then the family from the coast arrived to stay. They brought the furry dog with them again, and this time—much to Miss Sweetie's disgust—her mum let the dog come into the house and sit on her lap while the family was in the lounge room!!

Miss Sweetie was not happy!! While she loved having the little children to play with, the *dog* was just too much, especially her mum letting it sit on her lap!! So, in absolute disgust, Miss Sweetie went back and hid in the bedroom cupboard.

The very next morning, as her mum was getting ready to have her shower and get dressed for the day, Miss Sweetie climbed up onto the bathroom vanity to have a serious talk with her. Miss Sweetie was letting her know she was not happy about that dog!!

The family from the coast stayed for a little while, going up to the hospital, making sure Miss Sweetie's mum would eat, and they cleaned the house for her. All the family seemed sad.

A week passed and the family from the coast had to go back home. Miss Sweetie heard them all talking about her dad being sent to the big hospital in the city.

Over the next six weeks Miss Sweetie noticed her mum left the house early every day, and came home late in the evening. Sometimes her mum would just hop into her bed and cry. That is when Miss Sweetie knew she just needed to cuddle her mum.

Finally, after six long weeks, her dad was back home, and once again Miss Sweetie settled into being his nurse. She loved getting up to give him cuddles.

Miss Sweetie was vigilant, making sure her dad practiced walking again on the walker. This was the one part of being a good nurse she especially enjoyed, and Miss Sweetie settled into the routine of making sure her dad walked every day.

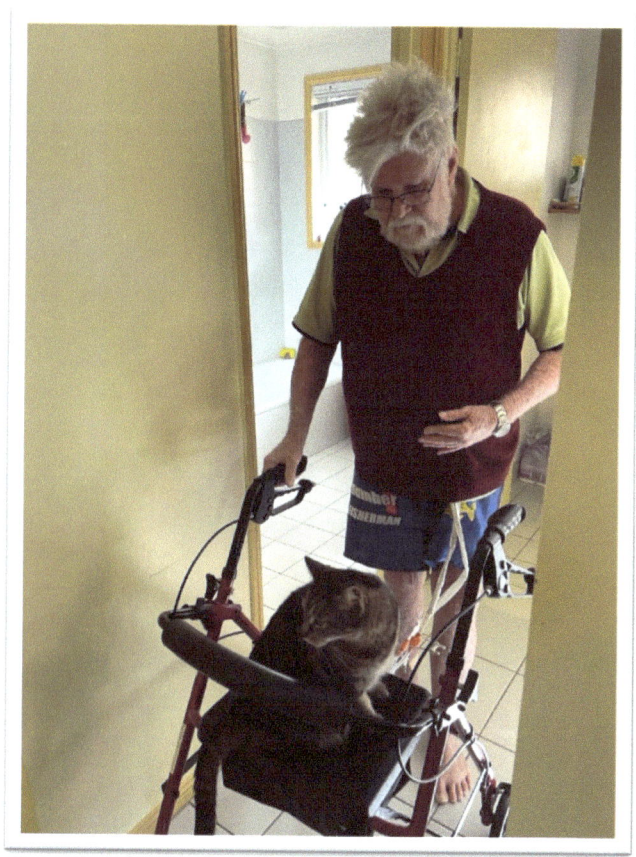

Miss Sweetie also kept a close eye on the nurses who came to look after her dad. She made sure they did things correctly.

But she spent most of the time sleeping on his lap—just glad her dad was home again safe and well.

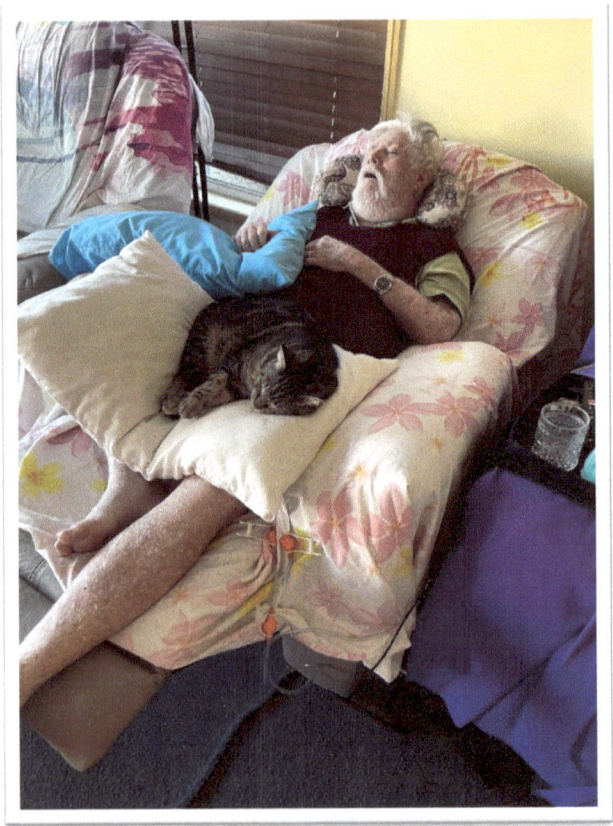

PART TWO

The Cat And The Housekeeper

It is going on four years now since our lovely Miss Sweetie arrived in our house. On the first Christmas after Miss Sweetie arrived our daughter gave me the sign:

'THE CAT AND ITS HOUSEKEEPER LIVE HERE'

What an intuitive statement! It is certainly true of the relationship Miss Sweetie and I have with each other. Boy, have I learnt my place!

From the moment Miss Sweetie entered our lives I knew she was here for a purpose, and that was to be a loving companion to my husband — she idolises him.

There is a saying:

'Dogs have masters and cats have slaves'.

How very true! Since I was fifteen years old, I have had the honour of being a servant to many of my feline friends.

I have learnt that they are very much independent individuals, and they have their own agenda — that is not necessarily yours!

What I Have Learned About Cats ...

Cats choose their owners

You may ask what I mean by this statement. I had a kitten once that I had rescued, and every day it would just disappear and then come back at night. I found out after a while that my kitty was going to visit an elderly lady three doors down to spend time with her.

She knew the cat belonged somewhere else so she would put the cat back out at night. Once I realised how attached my kitty and the lady were to each other, I made sure she went to her new home where they lived together happily.

Cats let you know if they are not happy

Cats have a particular way of letting you know they are not happy.

My husband and I found this out from Miss Sweetie the first time we had a visit from our children and our grand-dog, Diamond. Miss Sweetie was *not* happy, and she was so distressed that went to the toilet all over our bed.

We learnt this lesson really fast that day: to put Miss Sweetie's litter tray in our ensuite when we have visitors, until they go home. Cats are easily upset, and they will let you know by marking their territory: by either rubbing themselves on things or — in severe cases — by going to the toilet where you don't want them to.

Cats are fussy eaters

It doesn't matter if they liked a certain food last week, it does not mean they will like it today. My mother's cat was always fussy, and one day — in her absolute frustration — she said, "No way the blinking cat will eat what I have put down for it!" You guessed it, the cat refused to eat, and my mother gave in within the week.

This is also my challenge with our Miss Sweetie. If she has suddenly taken a dislike to something we have provided, she would rather go without than give in to what is on offer!

Cats sleep all day and explore at night

I always insist our cats stay in at night. But it doesn't stop the antics of our Miss Sweetie, running through the house like a mad thing.

She loves her balls! In fact, she is a feline soccer player, and under the couch—or the TV cabinet—are the goal posts. This results in us having to get down on the floor to get the balls back out ... or I just pick up more from the shops until the grandkids arrive again to help Granma retrieve them.

Cats have an intuitive nature

I have found with all of the cats I have known that they always knew when I was not well.

When my Tigger was alive, he would always climb up on my bed and put his paw on my forehead like he was taking my temperature. This is the same trait I have seen in our Miss Sweetie's nature, when it comes to my husband.

Lately, she comes to let me know if she is concerned about her dad, so I can go and check on him. She becomes very insistent, and won't stop yowling until I do what she wants. Each time she has had a valid reason to be concerned. I am forever grateful she is in our lives, keeping an eye on us both.

Miss Sweetie's favourite position—when in the lounge room with her mum and dad—is lying on her back, staring straight at them and blinking her eyes lovingly.

Miss Sweetie's Many Qualities ...

Miss Sweetie, the Office Assistant

Since my retirement from full-time work in 2021, my life has taken on a different role.

One of the first things I set about doing was to self-publish my first book, *Creating a Fond Farewell*, which resulted in Miss Sweetie deciding she needed to spend time in the office with me.

Sometimes it is a challenge to keep her out of mischief, and to stop her walking all over my keyboard ... especially now as she knows I am writing this book about her!

I do believe she is proud of my first effort, and I'm sure she would like to take credit for some of the work that went into the process of writing, editing, and printing the first copies!

Miss Sweetie, the Mischief Maker

Miss Sweetie is a tough foreman, and she likes to ensure I do the housework correctly. However, one day she got a little too enthusiastic. I was trying to find a particular book under my coffee table, which resulted in Miss Sweetie deciding she would help by pulling them *all* out, and then giving me the 'sweet innocent look'.

Or ... likewise when I am are trying to make the bed and she wants to pounce all over it, chasing my hands as I try to smooth the doona cover!

Or ... even when I am trying to do something on the iPad she has to get in the way and interrupt what I am doing!

Or ... just hiding in some random places to scare us when we are not looking!

One rule we have is that Miss Sweetie is not allowed on top of the kitchen table, but ... all bets are off if she thinks there is something to investigate!

Miss Sweetie also likes to tug on the clothes I hang up in our bathroom to dry. She is constantly checking things out.

When Miss Sweetie is in the wrong

Miss Sweetie knows when she has done something wrong, and she likes to put herself in 'time out'. This is achieved by hiding under the dining room chairs and looking innocently out at us ... almost as though she is in jail.

This cat does crack me up!

Here, she was still in the wrong, so she chose a different chair to put herself into 'time out'.

A cat's curiosity never stops …

Our Miss Sweetie likes to lie on my clothes when I am getting ready to go out somewhere.

Handbags or shoes on the floor? You can guarantee our Miss Sweetie will check them out — it is one of her favourite pastimes!

Miss Sweetie ... now the Office Manager!

Miss Sweetie is always on the job, whether it is taking over her mum's office, supervising the writing of books, or helping her dad out at his computer, it is a busy life for an office professional — always trying to keep us on our toes.

Miss Sweetie Finds A Home

Miss Sweetie at Play

As we learned earlier, one of Miss Sweetie's favourite pastimes is playing with things around the house, especially her colourful balls with the bells in the middle. Or chasing a piece of string and wrestling with her fluffy toys.

Miss Sweetie Finds A Home

Miss Sweetie also likes to get into mischief at Christmas time, whether it is chasing the elves, wrecking the Christmas tree, getting hold of the decorations ... or just pretending to be 'Santa Claws'.

When the day is done ...

Miss Sweetie manages to keep herself quite busy throughout the day, and when she isn't wandering around after me, or sleeping on the couch with her dad, sometimes she likes to snuggle up and go to sleep on my lap.

Miss Sweetie Finds A Home

From a bumpy start as an orphan, and after many adventures along the way, Miss Sweetie *absolutely* found her home ... and *definitely* became the heart of our family!

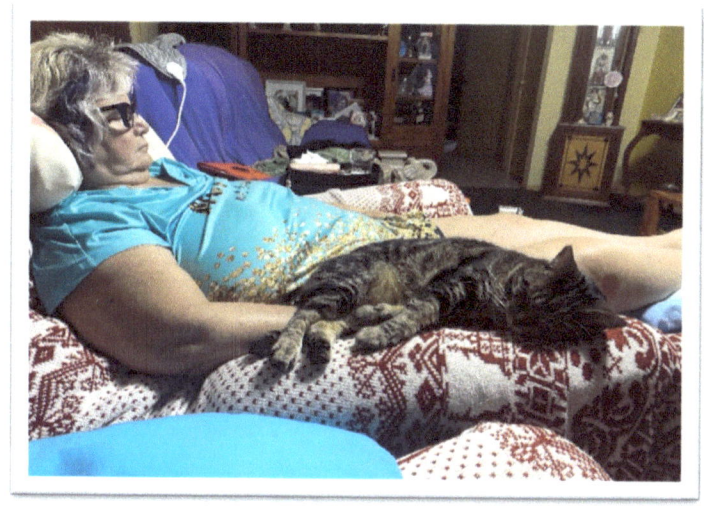

Oh yes, and she has now decided to be my friend!

About the Author

RITA-MARIE LENTON

Rita-Marie Lenton grew up in rural Queensland, Australia, and her own life story is one of triumph over adversity, and the gift of forgiveness.

Since retiring from her fascinating twenty-one-year career as a funeral director and crematorium manager, Rita-Marie's working world still involves life's rites of passage, but on a more spiritual and intuitive level, as a funeral and wedding celebrant.

Rita-Marie is a contributing author to a number of books and publications, and has also authored her own book, *Creating a Fond Farewell*, self-published on the Amazon platform.

From her residence on the beautiful Redcliffe Peninsula in Queensland, she has created her second book, *Miss Sweetie Finds A Home ... and becomes the heart of a family,* about her high-maintenance, and media-savvy rescue cat, Sweetie.

Certified through Doreen Virtue as an Angel Intuitive, when she isn't connecting with her angelic guides, Rita-Marie loves spending time with her family and continuing to follow the antics of her feline friend.

Acknowledgements

We are often asked what is our 'why'?

It is a good question, and one I have thought about often, especially when I set about doing something important.

I wanted to create a first-hand account of our journey with our rescue cat, Sweetie, whom I lovingly name "Miss Sweetie", with my tongue firmly in my cheek.

I wrote this book to draw attention to the remarkable work that Peninsula Animal Aid does, and to highlight the joy of adopting an older animal.

My book also explores the emotional connections between animal and owner, and the bonds they form.

I want to convey my personal thanks and appreciation to my dear friend, Fran Cahill, for writing such an insightful foreword.

To my other three wonderful friends, Albina Porracin, Di Riddell, and Peta-Ann Wood, for taking the time to read my book, offer feedback, and provide me with three gracious testimonials.

To my darling editor, Joanne Scott, what would I do without you? Thank you for taking the time and the effort to add in extra photos, and for being such a meticulous wordsmith, fixing my errors and correcting my spelling.

Last, but not least, my special thanks to Deborah Fay of Disruptive Publishing, and the Authorpreneurs Bootcamp, for being there every step of the way as I bumble along on my self-publishing journey.

Resources for animal rescue

Peninsula Animal Aid (Clontarf, Queensland)

https://peninsulaanimalaid.com.au/

RSPCA Queensland

www.rspcaqld.org.au/

RSPCA Australia

www.rspca.org.au/

Small Paws Pet Rescue

www.petrescue.com.au/groups/11493

More by the same Author

Rita-Marie Lenton is a contributing author to several compilation books in the intuitive genres of self-development, mental and emotional wellbeing, and spirituality.

See more from Rita-Marie in the following publications:

Touched by Breast Cancer
            compiled by Trish Springsteen

Forever Changed by Suicide
            compiled by Trish Springsteen

Lockdown Stories
Reflections on the pandemic from around the world
            compiled by Joanna O'Donoghue

Creating A Fond Farewell by Rita-Marie Lenton
Written from Rita-Marie's personal experiences within the funeral industry to share the art of saying a meaningful goodbye to a loved one.

Contact Rita-Marie Lenton

 www.facebook.com/Soulcrystalearth/

 www.instagram.com/soulcrystalearth_/?hl=en

 https://rita-marielenton.com.au/home

www.ingramcontent.com/pod-product-compliance
Lightning Source LLC
Chambersburg PA
CBHW042349300426
44109CB00035B/135